CINEMA OF *THE* *PRESENT*

LISA *ROBERTSON*

Coach House Books, Toronto

first edition, second printing, August 2021

Published with the generous assistance of the Canada Council for the Arts and the Ontario Arts Council. Coach House Books also acknowledges the support of the Government of Canada through the Canada Book Fund.

LIBRARY AND ARCHIVES CANADA CATALOGUING IN PUBLICATION

Robertson, Lisa, author
    Cinema of the present / Lisa Robertson.

Poems.
Issued in print and electronic formats.
ISBN 978-1-55245-297-4 (pbk.).

    I. Title.

PS8585.O3217C56 2014   C811'.54   C2014-904392-9

Cinema of the Present is available as an ebook: ISBN 978 1 77056 391 9

Purchase of the print version of this book entitles you to a free digital copy. To claim your ebook of this title, please email sales@chbooks.com with proof of purchase or visit chbooks.com/digital. (Coach House Books reserves the right to terminate the free digital download offer at any time.)

In addition, one must allow for chance discoveries, always possible in this vast domain in which the investigation has not been systematically pursued.

– Émile Benveniste

*W*hat is the condition of a problem if you are the problem?

You move into the distributive texture of an experimental protocol.

A bunch of uncanniness emerges.

At 20 hertz it becomes touch.

A concomitant gate.

At the middle of your life on a Sunday.

A dove, a crowned warbler in redwood, an alarm, it stops.

You set out from consciousness carrying only a small valise.

A downtown tree, the old sky, and still you want an inventory.

You were an intuition without a concept.

A gallery, a hospital, an hypothesis.

Pure gesture.

A gate made of carpet tape.

Even to prolixity you strayed.

A gate made of weatherproof tar.

Within the concept of the present, the figure-ground relationship effaced itself.

A gate made of a brick.

You are the silence they exchanged.

A gate made of a plinth.

It was a wide and empty Pacific place in too-strong light, with a general appearance of low-grade lack.

A gate made of a sofa bed and light bulbs.

You tried to see how the sky in 1972 comes up absent.

A gate made of artificial plants, vinyl, hinges and pins.

Smudgy, thick, cold.

A gate made of badminton shuttlecocks.

Is this a city?

A gate made of bejewelled barrettes, artificial peaches, a rotary phone.

And this too?

A gate made of bread and screws.

You believe women exist.

A gate made of buckets.

Nature mocks you.

A gate made of cotton, nylon, rubber and leather.

I see it on your face.

A gate made of exit signs, metal mesh, payroll sheets, chrome walkers.

I keep asking about the facts: tiredness, procrastination, doubt.

A gate made of floral foam, beeswax, silver leaf, drywall.

Each hormone curates something untenable.

A gate made of forceps and silicone tube.

There's no logic to what organisms demand.

A gate made of gas pumps.

You would educate yourself to an absolute and unconditional submission to the demands of transcription.

A gate made of gold, metal rods, driftwood, glass, concrete, peacock feathers, wood.

For you are such a procession.

A gate made of iron, neon, clay.

Only your tail was human.

A gate made of lamps.

Bark closed over your words.

A gate made of marble and coat-check stubs.

For you there is no information.

A gate made of medium-density fibreboard, fibreglass, foam, balsa wood and copper.

And at first you stank with the sensation of fate in your gut.

A gate made of Perspex.

And even a stab of love for your condition.

A gate made of photocopies, photographs, computer prints.

Irony was both your mother tongue and the intimate science of your future.

A gate made of photocopy.

Tell me more about animals, you said.

A gate made of poles, stanchions and masking tape.

Trash gyres, pre-objective monumentality, a rental.

A gate made of string and charcoal.

A gate made of photocopy.

A gate made of turntables.

When the anarchic excess has already been anticipated, what next?

A gate made of wood.

You might go so far as to falter.

A gate of hacksaw blades and bicycle spokes.

You sought a coat for intellectual ampleness.

A girl in a black cotton dress and bare legs is wearing a tiara.

Were you a dandy then?

A graph, a growth curve, an age pyramid, a distribution cloud; a palpability.

You, with your one-sided headache, your dark relationship to nature, your lack of whatever.

A jay, a rook, a parking ticket.

I don't know what you felt.

A latent rhythm discovered you.

Let us suppose that language is compatible with your errors.

A miniaturist, a Benedictine, a prisoner.

You sallied forth across emptied sidewalks, your fists in your pockets.

A quorum of crows will be your witness.

You're witnessing the belated eruption of a real condition.

A thumb-sized bird, a medieval allegory, a metaphor that sustains the activity of thinking.

It's already your life.

A university, a swimming pool, a botanical park.

A downtown tree, the old sky, and still you want an inventory.

About the time question in money culture: you perceive an exhausted narrative hardening into currency.

Unfortunately, all of your considerable skepticism was retroactive.

About the violet ethnicity: you've always been a dandy.

You had the sensation of bathing in doubt as if it were silence.

Again you consider the sumptuous wreckage of the present.

You re-emerged confused.

This is the economy of the psoas, economy of the engram, economy of vena cava, economy of unforgetting.

What if your only witness were an animal?

Against which you perceive a joyous unfounding.

I'm in debt to your radiant obscenity.

Ah, the true and fluent beauty of distant mass protest!

You were hubris and I liked this about you.

Ah, tiny experience.

I have not tried to remove the special objects of your scorn.

All day long and even in the night you built precise pictures of sensing.

You think this place could be worldless.

All you wanted was a little bit of accurate description in which to disappear.

You worked with painstaking fidelity to the documents.

Allotment machines, irises, lamps, water clocks, laws, indictments.

Your face was pure query.

Already the city you had described was gone.

Your concept remained surface but you didn't yet know why.

Also you have aspired to a sincerity of skepticism.

In the stain patterns on retail carpets you saw humans escaping themselves, deer braying to the God, Poussin demi-porn.

Always a war has been fought on your body.

You found music and pleasantness in the copula.

Always for you the present is wreckage, or it is the part of a science that does not yet exist.

This worn, preoccupied margin will be your vantage point.

Always you think it is over, when it is not.

Today, Thursday, the way people drift is your query.

An idyll in a bungalow; a palpability; a loss.

There's nothing you'd like to transfigure elsewhere.

An unknowing expands within your pronoun but it feels convivial.

Nothing apart from the gushing, bilious, abdicating live body.

And afternoon passes into evening with the usual ritual uncertainty, and you annotate the skyline making certain to include the word 'apricot.'

You made your muscles into extremely fine and silky tools.

And at first you stank with the sensation of fate in your gut.

What light did, how the trees freed it: these were among your topics.

And even a stab of love for your condition.

You seem to be an inversion in perception.

And I am walking in your garments.

A quorum of crows will be your witness.

And if you discover you were bought?

You note the smell of rain, bread and exhaust mixed with tiredness.

And if you yourself are incompatible with your view of the world?

And what is the subject but a stitching?

Once again you are the one who promotes artifice.

At 2 a.m. on Friday, you burn with a maudlin premonition.

And rankings and rankings and badges and repetitions.

You went with your friends to talk.

And so you hit upon your grandeur.

Maybe you do believe.

And the daily inversions of protocol.

They'll let you.

And the enjoyable gland also dribbles its politics.

In this way you come to understand the idea of destiny.

And the weeping was fed an earring.

It was a place like the farm, but near the ocean.

And then also: Jésuitique, De Chasse, En Valise, En Coquille, À la Colin, À la Paresseuse, À l'Italienne, À la Russe.

You were out somersaulting in darkness.

And then you recline against an image.

How difficult to choose between a system and a method!

And there you were, still in your travelling clothes.

You were being internally photographed.

And these phonemes were the phonemes of a perfume that combed your body.

Sometimes the concept of plenitude is a help.

And this is the continuous action of the given world on your person.

You pulled over to sleep.

And this too?

Very simply like this you disappeared into the interval.

And what is the subject but a stitching?

But you did not disappear to yourself.

And yet incomplete.

From the commuter train you felt the sensation of the brown river pulling the flat sky down toward it.

And you became subject to institutional curfews.

Glands, nerves, ligaments.

And you counted, you counted.

A gate made of photocopies, photographs, computer prints.

And you had a conceptual sensation.

Your stiff tail is all incipience.

And you have no money, but all of your cruelty is intact.

Thus a work begins.

And you itched.

The act's absurdity is balanced by its excess.

And you knew a lady who was irritated.

And you itched.

And you knew an alienated concept.

You wanted to release priorness.

And you knew of an antithetical expression.

Will it bring? Will it occupy? Is it simply sparkly?

And you know death has no image for it.

When you do it in your videos, you're female.

And you said, 'colouration.'

I'm entirely for your fucked-up way of living.

And you were falling out of this perfectly broken world.

You were finding out about the collapsible body.

And you yourself were not wholly able to resist the identification you had ridiculed.

The problem is not your problem.

And your despair is not a philosophic datum.

You rotate away from its sign.

Are you not both esoteric and practical?

There will be a period of measuring, testing and rebelling.

Are you rich?

Then there will be a period of exuding, celebrating and cheering.

Are you for garlands?

Then there will be the unknown period, the one you do not wish to represent.

As for the scrappy parking-lot trees, you are full of tenderness for the feminine in them.

What's natural, what's social, what's intuitive?

As for the serial description …

You now no longer use better words.

As in the difficult dream, you see a common roadside flower.

You say we clothe ourselves against death.

As years go by, you waste more and more value.

Tell me if you haven't had grief.

At 2 a.m. on Friday, you burn with a maudlin premonition.

You recalled the yellow flower called the cuckoo culled for luck in early spring.

At 20 hertz it becomes touch.

History is your nature.

At dusk the light through the black branches was enough.

I see it on your face.

At first you couldn't decide about style.

The wall itself is complicated, emotional.

At first you wanted only this tangible surplus.

Funny, cosmic and humble.

At fourteen and a half minutes, the sound of pages slowly turning, you note.

A gate made of badminton shuttlecocks.

At the edges of banality, there is sensing.

One out of three.

At the edges of sensing, no solution.

You had thrown yourself into risk without recognizing the act for what it was.

At times you had wanted only to float upon the norms of a beautiful language, obedient.

'To speak and to understand,' you said, 'this is difficult.'

At times you indulge in an ostentation of sorrow.

Instead, you'd posit a museum.

At times you love nastiness and bawdry.

The current place looks a lot like the world with its trees and houses, but, for example, when you wake up, there is only one bird, and then that bird stops.

At times you speak just for the fun of transience.

The delicate coyote, the streetlights, the pungent night.

Atoms, theatres, famines.

A gate made of turntables.

Authority is speech that does not limit itself to mimicking something that already exists; it is free to deform and invent, as long as it remains obedient to its own inner law, you read.

This city had the right to destroy you a little bit.

Bark closed over your words.

Through the non-sexual streets, through the redwoods with the little yellow light glancing about, through the small cluttered tables of the dark restaurant, in a blurry diagonal of tiny sounds – all very sensitive – then came life, feeling and forgetting.

Battlefields, cooking pots, medlars.

Then came an erotic thought: what if style were your only intelligibility?

Because it's not a site, it's a style, and it hurts.

You recalled the heaviness of blankets in the cabins of 1979.

Because of manners, textures, protocols, the shaking of cloth and the soft noise.

You recalled the driftwood windowsills and tumbling pine cones on the roofs.

Because of subjectivity, you said.

And the daily inversions of protocol.

Because you are lazy and voluptuous.

It was a place on a ruined map.

Because you could express yourself with her face it had become your face.

That morning in the hotel bed, you experienced your thinking as moving surfaces that intersected sequentially and at varying angles.

Beneath them the slithering black river.

Each conducts a kind of deeply described change.

Birdlet with the weight of a gasp.

Your internal sensation was that of a moving space of surfaces become soundlessly musical.

Black mould, animal hair, food, receipts, petals, sloughed skin.

Was this your hubris?

But duration isn't linear.

Your tradition: the dried-out green bottle fly dangling from a web like an earring.

But you are not Mademoiselle Falconetti's face.

The pools of bile on the floor of the operating theatre glinting beneath heavenly lamps.

But you did not disappear to yourself.

You rest just to the side of this great, innocent, manipulated faith in the individual will.

But you have not been educated to use it.

What is a pronoun but a metaphor?

But you'll wedge open the artificial and malleable caesura for a moment longer.

You'll see.

But your desire is not an instrument.

You become the girl who swims underwater.

But your theory of rest begins at the horizon.

Because you could express herself with her face it had become your face.

By means of description, a whole profound mass of time became your milieu.

You are insistent about the uncovering of this potential indifference.

Carnations and peat moss and a collapsing wall.

Who are you in relation to this woman?

Certainly you have aspired to thoroughness.

You feel minute perceptions speeding across a dirty surface.

Coded, highbrow, late-night.

Your subject shouldn't be rationed but expressed as the traversal of this surface.

Coming to this place, looking out over the passing container yards, the cranes like fractured Trojan animals, you are carved out by sadness, and roads, and the entire moving skin of history.

You wanted to see an image that had never been seen before.

Could it be over already?

Grief harms the spleen.

Could you be the historian of the future?

Speak, tiny expensive morning.

Curiosity, limbs and momentum: because of form you keep playing.

Expose yourself to the sensitive paper.

You're Cuvier smashing the glass jars at the Natural History Museum.

You aren't a woman.

Didn't it seem that earth believed you?

Here is a hut surrounded by improvised flags on chain-link: everything is potential in it.

Don't warn us again. Don't toot the little horns.

This is where thinking could become nature, where both are only incomplete.

Each conducts a kind of deeply described change.

Coming to this place, looking out over the passing container yards, the cranes like fractured Trojan animals, you are carved out by sadness, and roads, and the entire moving skin of history.

Each has a horoscope.

Such facts lie beneath the grasp of contemporary research.

Each hormone curates its procession.

The way you practice emergence is through longing.

Each of the several rhythmic sequences remains intransigent, and so you make thought with them.

You shook 'til the little harness flew from your face.

Enough of laboriousness! you cry.

Socius rex.

Even the distant hum of cars from the highway overpass.

What's worse, you are usually prematurely grateful.

Even to prolixity you strayed.

One part of you after another catches fire.

Even your tears were rhythmic.

But duration isn't linear.

Expose yourself to the sensitive paper.

Once again you were a girl in a foreign park struggling to read Nietzsche.

Feminism wants to expand the sensorium.

You tried to remember each hotel room in each town and city and the view from each window over strange and happy roofs and streets.

Flanking the clatter and shriek of migrations, the silence of slow rotting.

You would visit the great libraries just prior to their destruction in order to taste the ancient ego nectar.

For a moment you were the indispensable horizon of all that occurs or appears.

You said you can't evade a binary by turning.

For example, in the noticed friction between thinking and perceiving, your provocation could be built.

You are at the same time descriptive and argumentative.

For how long do you mean to be contingent?

Still, at this late date in the political, you remain intrigued by fucking.

For me alone you have eroticized Aristotle.

And you yourself were not wholly able to resist the identification you had ridiculed.

For so long now you have wanted me to do this for you, quietly.

Because of manners, textures, protocols, the shaking of cloth and the soft noise.

For you are such a procession.

Yes, the lateness was not of the body but of the city.

For you there is no information.

You liked to carry out partial recuperations because they were less plausible.

For you, rhetoric and erotics are irreparably aligned and give support to a needed life.

You have been accused of being a pornographer.

For you, subjectivity would be about inventing a populated world that exists.

If you have rarely tried to speak of it, it's because form requires of you a reticence.

Free error is what you'd call it.

And I am walking in your garments.

From the commuter train you had noted the sensation.

Nor must you eliminate contradictions.

From your mouth issues a varied stream of flowers: roses, columbines and others.

What do you believe about form?

Funny, cosmic and humble.

You resound elsewhere.

Gently you press the time of the quotidian all over its surface.

You became successively a priest, a gambler, a thief, apprentice to an apothecary, a doctor, a clerk in a provincial town.

Glands, nerves, ligaments.

For a moment you are the indispensable horizon of all that occurs or appears.

Grief harms the spleen.

There must be several distinct kinds of ephemerality, you decide.

Grumblingly.

You offer your substance to an interpretive intervention.

Here is your hut.

You were standing outside in your body.

History is your nature.

In the dream you were conducting a symphonic grid of sleep, which was both your own sleep scattered and the sleep of others.

How are you distributed across negation?

You were out in a paper boat in the river of the city, listening,

How did you come to be in the vicinity of these sunken pools and chandeliers?

To construct a velocity is what you want.

How difficult to choose between a system and a method!

You're interested in the brutality of description: it is the traversal of this infinitely futile yet fundamental and continuous space called the present.

How do you conserve the memory of these actions?

In eight hours you saw it become a world assaulted by truth and medicine.

How does it look?

Your problem is again your own transformation.

How does that work?

You couldn't again submit your own name.

How else do you construct a pause in cognition?

But you'll wedge open the artificial and malleable caesura for a moment longer.

How many indices must you write?

You could never decide about will and using it.

I can't do a thing when I am in your presence.

Your new skin would be prosodic – that is, both esoteric and practical.

I don't know how to solve your loneliness.

You are a transitional figure who sees yourself as such.

I don't know what you felt.

With ruffles cascading from shoulders.

I found five hundred solid and nervous words in the margin of your Johnson.

No throbbing sea behind you.

I have not tried to remove the special objects of your scorn.

Your fluid would be spit.

I independently share your priorities.

Yours is the prosody of being misapprehended. It has been called shame and has a conventional pronoun.

I keep asking about the facts: tiredness, procrastination, doubt.

You abandon it here.

I knew you in your exquisite moment.

At the edges of banality, there is sensing.

I must not believe that you judge on the basis of facts; you judge on the basis of what you are.

You became strange, you became my eyes.

I put my studies at your disposition.

You see small mammals fighting in trees.

I see it on your face.

Periodically a building will produce an exoskeleton of great vulnerability.

I see it on your face.

Is this the surface where expression converts to love?

I, Byronic, you said, screwed my way forward.

You were reading the city recklessly.

I'm entirely for your fucked-up way of living.

Of shapely pleasure you spoke.

I'm for the ennoblement of your curious kind of existence.

You came to understand the idea of destiny in this way.

I'm in debt to your radiant obscenity.

Thus you were led to describe hospitals, prisons, remote villages, monasteries.

If I want to cry it's because I'm not a pessimist, you said.

You conducted the documentation of a trembling.

If life is your idea, it's an idea with fur.

At fourteen and a half minutes, the sound of pages slowly turning, you note.

If you have rarely tried to speak of it, it's because form requires of you a reticence.

A dove, a crowned warbler in redwood, an alarm, it stops.

If you paint with a blushy tint, it's mostly kept for solitary pleasures: napping, smoking, strolling, thieving.

A gate made of iron, neon, clay.

If you speak in this imaginary structure, it's because other choices felt limiting.

Perfection in three tracks plus refrigerator motor.

In eight hours you felt it become a world assaulted by truth and medicine.

Enough of laboriousness! you cry.

In expressive range too, your atmosphere branched out.

You're in favour of a potent inhumanness.

In order to enter you needed an identity.

But you have not been educated to use it.

In the aristocracy of interventions you walked.

You think with plants and rags, with prepositional inadequacy, with improvised throat of sorrow.

In the dream you were conducting a symphonic grid of sleep, which was both your own sleep scattered and the sleep of others.

Didn't it seem that earth believed you?

In the old clothes market you witnessed your own unravelling.

Maybe your resistance came over you like a dream.

In the old studio photograph your lipstick is black.

You awoke and boiled your dress in ink.

In the shabbiness of persisting, the lapsed fibres and the dust, you find an economy to achieve.

With such amplitude you became impersonal.

In the stain patterns on retail carpets you saw humans escaping themselves, deer braying to the God, Poussin demi-porn.

By means of description, a whole profound mass of time became your milieu.

In this way you are a purveyor of doubt.

And you had a conceptual sensation.

In this way you are motility.

It was then that 'the body' unhooked your mind.

Inextricably you arrive at a weak argument. Impeccably, that is.

O, Rosy-booted.

Inside a taxonomy it quivers and variegates.

What is the emotion of wit?

Instead you'll synthesize time.

A gallery, a hospital, an hypothesis.

Instead you posit a museum.

A gate made of bread and screws.

Intransigence, difficulty and unresolved contradiction.

I put my studies at your disposition.

Irony was both your mother tongue and the intimate science of your future.

Only you.

Is this a city?

It's tattersall, canvas, herringbone, Donegal, sateen, velour, felt, taffeta, percale, corduroy, shantung, crepe, twill, broadcloth, flannel, chiffon, gingham, velvet, velveteen, satin, gauze, piqué, melton, denim, worsted or nothing, you said.

Is this the surface where expression converts to love?

I knew you in your exquisite moment.

It billows lavishly from a narrowness.

What will you do next?

It falls to your knees.

What you wanted: total gestural plasticity, and to be perfumed by
something.

It is cause for celebration.

This would be your health.

It is still only noon in your reading.

Your projects and their wrecks and ruins; your dogs.

It is the country you are constrained to become.

The remarkable difficulty of compiling a secular index!

It occurs in the smallest possible space.

For so long now you have wanted me to do this for you, quietly.

It remains unachieved.

You are sometimes a confusion of formal levels and sometimes a
vicious circle.

It seems that your data does that.

You are a position effect.

*It takes you a long time to shed the specificity of your desires; in actuality
the task remains unfinished.*

Repose, now symbolized by the hour of noon, being the hinge for
your discussion.

It took you some time to discover the displacement.

Curiosity, limbs and momentum: because of form you kept playing.

It was a burning mortal agony, an insult.

A gate made of medium-density fibreboard, fibreglass, foam, balsa wood and copper.

It was a kind of dance music from the plains you hear at nighttime from far above.

You are fundamentally forgotten and veiled or you are deeply erased and diverted.

It was a place like the farm, but near the ocean.

You were poverty shivering in an old turquoise city.

It was a place of brutal mobility.

You need a hat against anger.

It was a place on a ruined map.

You send them back to their diminutive need to identify with every-thing they see.

It was a wide and empty Pacific place in too-strong light, with a general appearance of low-grade lack.

You are bitter gentian, gentian yellow.

It was not your voice at all, but it can't stop nor does it think.

You think that houses seem to be built entirely of sorrow.

It was spoken, transmitted, temporal, not arbitrary.

You presuppose a free, opened and unlimited space.

It was then that 'the body' unhooked your mind.

How does it look?

It's a low-slung rising of a kind of beneficial smoke in the chest.

You move to the left of the audible range of sound: pine wind in 1800s.
Winter night in 1700s. Crickets.

It's already your life.

And there you are, still in your travelling clothes.

It's just not true.

You carried the great discovery of poetry as freedom, not form.

It's just past noon on a Sunday.

This is what you look like.

*It's tattersall, canvas, herringbone, Donegal, sateen, velour, felt, taffeta,
percale, corduroy, shantung, crepe, twill, broadcloth, flannel, chiffon,
gingham, velvet, velveteen, satin, gauze, piqué, melton, denim, worsted
or nothing, you said.*

It falls to your knees.

It's time for your late style.

If I want to cry it's because I'm not a pessimist, you said.

Its immateriality is spoken, transmitted, temporal, not arbitrary.

The set of your mind returned uncertainty to the conventions of intimacy.

Its pronoun plays a social rupture.

You fling open regret.

Its scale will be wrong in order to announce an illegitimacy.

You are paid the compliment of being dreamt of.

Just violence and passivity and patience.

Thus you become the biographer of an opinion.

Landscapes, speakers, furniture.

All day long and even in the night you built precise pictures of existing.

Last night the parking lot was dreaming the words of your ancestors and enemies.

In this way you are a purveyor of doubt.

Let feminism be this girl raging at a chandelier.

A miniaturist, a Benedictine, a prisoner.

Let us suppose that language is compatible with your errors.

A concomitant gate.

Like sense you are anonymous.

You thought that you could take all of the risks.

Lingering is what you like.

Yet you remain unconvincing in your use of the word 'sex.'

Maybe your resistance came over you like a dream.

It was a place of brutal mobility.

Met, talked, disbanded, leaving no organizational trace.

It was not your voice at all, but it can't stop nor does it think.

Midway along that line that marks the adjacency of description to perception you paused.

You seized the freedom to occupy a vanishing referent.

More collective cosmetics! you decide.

This is what it looks like.

Nature mocks you.

Even your tears were rhythmic.

No theory is your life, Precious.

Who dreamt in Latin anyhow?

No throbbing sea behind you.

You went out into orality to purchase a pencil.

Nor are you the custodian of an image.

You left a wake of linguistic sillage.

Nor is sensing private.

And you became subject to institutional curfews.

Nor must you eliminate contradictions.

And you knew a lady who was irritated.

Nor were you fearful of the caesura.

And you knew an alienated concept.

Nothing apart from the gushing, bilious, abdicating live body.

And you knew an antithetical expression.

Now for you no open weeping.

And you were falling out of this perfectly broken world.

Now listening will be the luminous duration of your tissues.

Perfectly broken.

Now only time is wild.

You counted into the problem.

Now to enact comically solemn rituals, you said.

You didn't die.

Now you know that all along it's been the body that you can't understand.

Sedately and ceaselessly you continued to elaborate the barest premise.

Now you must return by a different route.

You have other doctrines.

Now you wanted only to make an immodest document.

What city are you seeing?

Now you would be a governess perhaps, with ink-spotted sheets and frayed lingerie.

You are in a world of plurals – shops, offices, lamps and subways.

Now you'll be a whore, now you'll say 'darling.'

About the time question in money culture: you perceive an exhausted narrative hardening into currency.

O Sir, you said, had I only been able to tell a quarter of what I saw and felt beneath that tree.

You have invented nothing.

O, Rosy-booted.

A university, a swimming pool, a botanical park.

Of shapely pleasure you spoke.

A gate of hacksaw blades and bicycle spokes.

On a level with intuitive reason and the complicated history of grace.

Within the intensity of waiting you see foliage and its lights, you see extraordinary and calm people clearing tables.

Once again and with mild exhilaration you acquire a new surface.

The unachieved is the place that you call meaning.

Once again you were a girl in a foreign park struggling to read Nietzsche.

It is the country you are constrained to become.

One out of three.

You arrive at its diagram, accompanied by a strong aroma of melancholy.

One part of you after another catches fire.

Your formal discretion expressed itself in the non-convergence of identity with itself.

Only the rhyme transforms you.

Now you know what the body is.

Only you.

When irritated, you may form an hypothesis.

Only your tail was human.

Two identical melodic patterns fall out of sequence.

Out of curiosity you constructed a model.

Owls and lynxes; harts and bears; dogs, apes and vultures.

Owls and lynxes; harts and bears; dogs, apes and vultures.

A gate made of exit signs, metal mesh, payroll sheets, chrome walkers.

Paperback Iliad *on the dashboard.*

How do you conserve the memory of these actions?

Part of your immodesty is opaque.

You play and believe within a recurrent sensation.

Partly vibrant, partly wavering, partly failing.

You build a catalogue of depletions.

Perfection in three tracks plus refrigerator motor.

Such aesthetics are as unthinkable to you as they are necessary: memory and the present are not in opposition.

Perfectly broken.

The pleasure in leaving those quiet rooms!

Perhaps memory is a surface of negative curvature, you muse.

You receive a similar paucity.

Perhaps you are the memory of her senses.

You would like thought to release something other than laboratory conditions.

Periodically a building will produce an exoskeleton of great delicacy.

Using your lungs and her memory, you describe the ineffable boat.

In this way you come to understand the idea of destiny.

You're also collecting an archive of the absurdity of value.

Prosody was the house you sketched around your body.

A graph, a growth curve, an age pyramid, a distribution cloud; a palpability.

Pure gesture.

A gate made of a brick.

Repose, now symbolized by the hour of noon, being the hinge for your discussion.

You're the most imitative of all.

Rhythm itself speculates.

Your pronoun leaks thus.

Sedately and ceaselessly you continued to elaborate the barest premise.

You are then hostile and alien.

Shabbiness, fumbling, elbow grease.

Met, talked, disbanded, leaving no organizational trace.

Sheet lightning and large-dropped summer rain in short forays, 5 a.m.

You are a structure of comportment.

Similarly, that is.

With your languid pose, your elbow against a tree, your flute and your costume cut into diamond shapes.

Simultaneously for and against this tradition of minor failure, you have acquired a cummerbund.

You said we have both a colony and a god.

Smudgy, thick, cold.

To spare myself I'm going to drop these, you said.

So long, big doors, painted with sea light and honey.

To spare yourself the trouble you'll explore beginner infinities.

So now you are an economist.

You meant that by remarkably indirect paths you'd understand one god simply in order to let go of all belief.

So you came to nilling.

If life is your idea, it's an idea with fur.

So you sent for some novels.

Sheet lightning and large-dropped summer rain in short forays, 5 a.m.

Socius rex.

Your misunderstanding stopped just short of thoroughness and this was your particular charm.

Some believe you ought to assume a tone of sincerity.

It occurs in the smallest possible space.

Some have deep apartments, some have shallow apartments.

An idyll in a bungalow; a palpability; a loss.

Sometimes the concept of plenitude is a help.

A gate made of floral foam, beeswax, silver leaf, drywall.

Sometimes you need a record of your life.

How else do you construct a pause in cognition?

Speak, tiny expensive morning.

Grumblingly.

Still there was no solution for the fabulous problem.

With late style.

Still, at this late date in the political, you remain intrigued by fucking.

It's time for your late style.

Still, you're totally in love with subjectivity.

Midway along that line that marks the adjacency of description to perception you paused.

Such aesthetics are as unthinkable to you as they are necessary: memory and the present are not in opposition.

You had more important things to do.

Such facts lie beneath the grasp of contemporary research.

At the edges of sensing, there is banality.

Such that flowers, skulls, tables, subvert the vanitas.

You craved the diurnal irregularities of the imagining life.

Supernatural, social and divine.

You sensed your future unfounding.

Tattered Europe caking up in corners of abandoned rooms.

Your goodness lifts like a cock.

Tell me if you haven't had grief. Whatever grief is becoming.

You adore its heavy beauty.

Tell me more about animals, you said.

Free error is what you'd call it.

Temporary benevolent peripheries.

You burst to a skirty froth.

Was it enough?

You play and believe.

That love happened at all.

And so you hit upon your grandeur.

That morning in the hotel bed, you experienced your thinking as moving surfaces that intersected sequentially and at varying angles.

Then you lapsed in its observance.

That only your lovely arrogance permitted this.

You use speech to decorate duration for somebody. You stop just before it becomes a shape.

That the snow prevented you.

Because it's not a site, it's a style, and it hurts.

That they become their deaths, you said.

Very easy and very desperate.

That year, all of your muscles became useful.

There you were, kissing gratefully near water because you could.

That your mouth lovingly damaged the language.

You went to the river just to gaze at the river, like an old man.

The act's absurdity is balanced by its excess.

And you counted, you counted, you counted.

The balance changes, and you care less.

You almost thought.

The countess of prose in your abandoned orchard.

You said the market doesn't merit belief.

The current place looks a lot like the world with its trees and houses, but, for example, when you wake up, there is only one bird, and then that bird stops.

You wanted to make your tiredness into a surface.

The delicate coyote, the streetlights, the pungent night.

The houses you lived in, their porches, the bored women and girls working at the arena snack bars.

The description takes over the inchoate category.

Where else can you think change?

The dry tree of your task, the citydogs cavorting.

You breathed for those who dedicated themselves to burning.

The feeling of your sex became more and more mysterious.

What's the good of burning?

The form never extinguishes its own irony.

You are neutral, like an event.

The girl at the park fanning her hair in the sun.

Two doves in the pine; three, and a train; one gone and a dog in honey-suckle: how are you to make choices when perceiving is arbitrary?

The grand law empties you of preference.

You moved the taxonomy around.

The houses you lived in, their porches, the bored women and girls working at the arena snack bars.

Then you felt lyric obscenity, both erotic and rhetorical.

The huge sky over the working harbour felt home-like.

You had fallen upon the situation where the designation 'speculative' functioned as insult.

The I-speaker on your silken rupture spills into history.

Feminism wants to expand the sensorium.

The overpass hums in you all night as you sleep.

Once again and with mild exhilaration you acquire a new surface.

The peculiar indwelling of rime was a roving organ.

In the old studio photograph your lipstick is black.

The perceiving is for yourself, but meets at no doctrine of the subject.

You'd rather be a dandy than a writer.

The pleasure in leaving those quiet rooms!

O Sir, you said, had I only been able to tell a quarter of what I saw and felt beneath that tree.

The pools of bile on the floor of the operating theatre glinting beneath heavenly lamps.

Now you know that all along it's been the body that you don't understand.

The present is all with you.

You won't assume that in your century the darkness is necessary.

The problem is not your problem.

Your historical pleasure was metrically interrupted by the inadequacies of terminology.

The problem of solitude, what was it to you?

At dusk the light through the branches was enough.

The question for you becomes what are we doing with our bodies?

You haven't enough time to believe anything but the comedy of sensing.

The question now, you think, is who can really afford this law.

Such that flowers, skulls, tables, subvert the vanitas.

The remarkable difficulty of compiling a secular index!

Rhythm itself speculates.

The set of your mind returned uncertainty to the conventions of intimacy.

There you would be human.

The term has the sense of a prohibition.

Against which you perceive a joyous unfounding.

The thick scent of dust in the heat.

Its pronoun was a social sculpture.

The wall itself is complicated, emotional.

Like sense you are anonymous.

The way you experience emergence is through longing.

The girl at the park fanning her hair in the sun.

The whole density of life arrives in your forehead.

With no scarcity.

The whole shirred surface splitting and churning.

You went toward the great experimenters in the domain of longing.

Then came an erotic thought: what if style were your only intelligibility?

You frequent whatever's supernatural, negative and sexual.

Then pleasure afresh, pleats, strong buttocks.

It was a burning mortal agony, an insult.

Then psychology reared its battered head.

Thus your data shimmers.

Then sleepiness came like an incision.

You wore the dress as payment for entrance to the symbolic order.

Then there will be a period of exuding, celebrating and cheering.

How does it look?

Then there will be the unknown period, the one you do not wish to represent.

You're in a life-facing position.

Then you are occupied by a question.

You're fierce, then you're tired.

Then you are the memory of her dress.

This is how it looks.

Then you are thrown headlong into transcendent things.

What would you pay for it?

Then you felt lyric obscenity, both erotic and rhetorical.

Wore flowers at the spine.

Then you keep spilling.

You are a theatre, not a machinery.

Then you lapsed in its observance.

You are not a colour without having the colour of this red.

Then you penned a quick imitation on the freedom of stupidity.

You have here an unfixed being.

Then you were a student of the whole madness of painting.

For you, rhetoric and erotics are irreparably aligned and give support to a needed life.

Then you would be part of the science that does not yet exist.

Only the rhyme of discourse transforms you.

Thence to measured earth.

Landscapes, speakers, furniture.

There are a few brave people, but where are they?

A gate made of weatherproof tar.

There at the creature-riven unfounding, at the sorrow of animals, at the invention of sentiments.

You are freed from myself.

There has to be a procedure that doesn't involve shame but still has sound.

They seem to be engrossed in tiny acts of survival, you think.

There must be several distinct kinds of ephemerality, you decide.

You dream of the cogito, wanting to swim in its work.

There was light coming out of your skin.

For how long do you mean to be contingent?

There you go, there you go, there you go.

You'll cause the privative skit called sex.

There you look for what is already institutionally incomplete.

Lingering is what you like.

There you were, kissing gratefully near water because you could.

Then you are occupied by a question.

There you would be human.

There has to be a procedure that doesn't involve shame but still has sound.

There's an intimacy you want to protect.

The whole density of life arrives in your forehead.

There's no logic to what organisms demand.

Always you think it is over, when it is not.

There's nothing you'd like to transfigure elsewhere.

What you felt, as if all at once, was simply the open sensation of spaciousness.

Therefore you transcribed yourself.

Then you are thrown headlong into transcendent things.

These new fashions could help you feel hope.

Temporary benevolent peripheries.

They have wrapped the industrial ductwork in filmy mauve gauze.

Your sky crumbles open.

They seem to be engrossed in tiny acts of survival, you think.

A latent rhythm discovered your pronoun.

They'll let you.

The whole shirred surface splitting and churning.

This city had the right to destroy you a little bit.

The thick scent of dust in the heat.

This is different than saying language is volition.

And rankings and rankings and badges and repetitions.

This is how it looks.

Now for you no open weeping.

This is one part of a new level.

You'll build a support for the certainty of causelessness, for whatever is not the market, for the crane lowering the materials into irreality.

This is the annotation of the movement of the site of authority, you think.

You always describe potential with your body.

This is the continuous action of the given world.

To think in a bed in a hotel in an unfamiliar city is your dream.

This is what pouring looks like.

Your errors are colossal.

This is what you recognize.

You walked beside the wresting and burning of commodities.

This is where thinking could become nature, where both are only incomplete.

In the aristocracy of interventions you walked.

This protocol will show that newness is one of the possible horizons of forgetting.

You want a sonic socio-affective structure.

This worn, preoccupied margin will be your vantage point.

You are for the vocable.

This would be your health.

Are you not both esoteric and practical?

Then came life, feeling and forgetting.

I, Byronic, you said, screwed my way forward.

Thus a work begins.

What will you do with all that information?

Thus an hypothesis occurs to you: consciousness is cosmetic, but not in an individual sense.

You diligently study the subtext of the 2 a.m. conversation.

Thus the licking and sleeking of offices.

What about giving me the recipe for the strong scent of the world?

Thus you become the biographer of an opinion.

You simply contemplate those russet mountainsides.

Thus you were led to describe hospitals, prisons, remote villages, monasteries.

The description takes over the inchoate category.

Thus your data shimmers.

You are quite familiar with the iterative terrain.

Time is short; you need to constrain your feeling for the sentence.

Its pronoun plays a social rupture.

To construct a velocity is what you want.

You knew that already, but had once again forgotten.

To spare myself I'm going to drop these, you said.

At times you had wanted only to float upon the norms of a beautiful language, obedient.

To spare yourself the trouble you'll explore beginner infinities.

Wills, contracts and other such documents.

To think in a bed in a hotel in an unfamiliar city is your dream.

You had wanted to believe that language needs us to witness its time.

To whom do you speak?

You are its immaterial organ.

Today, Wednesday, the way people drift is your query.

So you sent for some novels.

Trash gyres, pre-objective monumentality, a rental.

Because of subjectivity, you said.

Trees, lights, on a level with the genitalia.

Tattered Europe caking up in corners of abandoned rooms.

Two doves in the pine; three, and a train; one gone and a dog in honeysuckle.

Then you were a student of the whole madness of painting.

Two identical melodic patterns fall out of sequence.

You swam into splendidness.

Unfortunately, all of your considerable skepticism was retroactive.

You knew what an animal is.

Unmotivated by any bodily narrative, you made one from the stuff at hand.

You say your health has never been written.

Unsorted, unparsed.

What will you be, then?

Using your lungs and her memory, you describe the ineffable boat.

That late morning of wind in mid-October, when you decided to live for your thinking – did it change anything?

Usually you will not have made a decision about how to advance.

You refuse apocalyptic consciousness.

Very easy and very desperate.

You bite into the fruit you invent and it runs down your face.

Very simply like this you disappeared into the interval.

You'll just speak for prosody from now on.

Vicious, vicarious shifters!

In this way you are motility.

Was this your hubris?

This is different than saying language is volition.

Were you a dandy then?

Your surface is entirely concentric.

What about giving me the recipe for the strong scent of the world?

You asked about love.

What are the conditions of a problem, if you are the problem?

It was a kind of dance music from the plains you hear at nighttime from far above.

What city are you seeing?

Ah, the true and fluent beauty of distant mass protest!

What do you believe about form?

And yet incomplete.

What if there were a life that sustains life?

You had drunk only half of the wine.

What if your only witness were an animal?

The problem of solitude, what was it to you?

What is a pronoun but a metaphor?

You're bent to a book as the uprising unfurls.

What is the emotion of wit?

You are the crow on Saint Radegund's desk.

What light did, how the trees freed it: these were among your topics.

You wanted to say something new about space and forests.

What we have is a mix of improper disclosures of partial information mixed with inaccurate information and then drawn into unfounded conclusions, you said.

You are provisional and unconcerned with the entire feminine machinery.

What will you be, then?

You're absolutely in love with trees.

What will you do next?

Each has a horoscope.

What will you do when you're human?

You entered this university of vines and crumpled mosaic, hot sun, the cracks in the walls, the balconies peeling and collapsed.

What will you do with all that information?

Your thinking is not a market.

What works then? What works?

You're for the viable infinity of the pelvis.

What would you pay for it?

I independently share your priorities.

What you felt was the movement of sound through your body in its bed in the city not your own but particular nonetheless.

Battlefields, cooking pots, medlars.

What you felt, as if all at once, was simply the open sensation of spaciousness.

A gate made of gas pumps.

What you got was a winter fur in summer.

You did this gravely.

What you see are muzzled speeches and political beliefs.

Yours is the social class that left.

What you wanted: total gestural plasticity, and to be perfumed by something.

There are a few brave people, but where are they?

What's natural, what's social, what's intuitive?

Flanking the clatter and shriek of migrations, the silence of slow rotting.

What's the good of burning?

You weep into a hand.

What's worse, you are usually prematurely grateful.

But you are not Mademoiselle Falconetti's face.

When the anarchic excess has already been anticipated, what next?

What will you do when you're human?

When you do it in your videos, you're female.

The term has the sense of a prohibition.

Where else can you think change?

Inside a taxonomy it quivers and variegates.

Wherever you go, you will be a city.

The question for you becomes what are we doing with our bodies, why are we here?

Who are you in relation to this woman?

You agreed, finally, to recognize and believe; then you reneged on the agreement.

Who dreamt in Latin anyhow?

You are only lyrical if you're harsh.

Who will describe your odd survival?

And if you yourself are incompatible with your view of the world?

Who will show you the secret to this living as a body?

This is one part of a new level.

Will it bring? Will it occupy? Is it simply sparkly?

In order to enter, you needed an identity.

Wills, contracts and other such documents.

Unmotivated by any bodily narrative, you made one from the stuff at hand.

Windshield wipers, train crossings, tape loops.

As in the difficult dream, you see a common American flower.

With late style.

You ask: what if language is already beyond itself?

With no scarcity.

You had been hoping for a quarter of an orange.

With ruffles cascading from shoulders.

You had been hoping for better questions.

With seemingly insufficient means, you slept, you wrote, you listened.

What you got was a winter fur in summer.

With such amplitude you became impersonal.

Then pleasure afresh, pleats, strong buttocks.

With the emotional artifice you share with all your class, you step off the curb.

A gate made of bejewelled barrettes, artifical peaches, a rotary phone.

With the immediacy of an iamb, you hear a child, a goose, a crow.

And if you discover you were bought?

With your hands in the pockets of your monumental coat, you strolled across the pedantry of becoming.

That your mouth lovingly damaged the language.

With your languid pose, your elbow against a tree, your flute and your costume cut into diamond shapes.

That only your lovely arrogance permitted this.

Within taxonomy, it quivers and variegates.

That love happened at all.

Within the concept of the present, the figure-ground relationship effaced itself.

It's time for the prosody of noise.

Within the intensity of waiting.

You can't go back.

Wore flowers at the spine.

This is the continuous action of the given world on your body.

Yeah, fleece and honey.

If you speak in this imaginary structure, it's because other choices felt limiting.

Yes, the lateness was not of the body but of the city.

The feeling of your sex became more and more mysterious.

Yet you experience your body as the failing and pulsing civic medium.

You thought of kinds of furnishings no longer popular, accumulating in cold barns and warehouses.

Yet you remain unconvincing in your use of the word 'sex.'

They have wrapped the industrial ductwork in filmy mauve gauze.

You abandon it here.

And you said, 'colouration.'

You adore its heavy beauty.

You believe you are of supple character.

You agreed, finally, to recognize and believe; then you reneged on the agreement.

You have retained most of your original arrogance.

You almost thought.

For me alone you have eroticized Aristotle.

You also have a theory for your saunter.

Ah, tiny experience.

You also take into consideration an element of rarity.

You are not the emergency of money.

You always describe potential with your body.

Yours was a shabby time, and you felt it as such.

You appropriate yourself into the distributive texture of an experimental protocol.

But your desire is not an instrument.

You are a position effect.

The balance shifts, and you care less.

You are a structure of comportment.

You are Lucretian and self-reliant but sometimes exhausted.

You are a theatre, not a machinery.

And you know death has no image for it.

You are a transitional figure who sees yourself as such.

Just violence and passivity and patience.

You are arrogant.

You saw the shadow of the hummingbird and then the hummingbird, from beneath.

You are at the same time descriptive and argumentative.

At times you speak just for the fun of transience.

You are banality.

Your differential was necessary.

You are bitter gentian, gentian yellow.

You had believed and argued for each of the theories in its turn.

You are for the vocable.

Now you wanted only to make an immodest document.

You are freed from myself.

Birdlet with the weight of a gasp.

You are fundamentally forgotten and veiled or you are deeply erased and diverted.

How many indices must you write?

You are in a world of plurals.

Always a war has been fought on your body.

You are insistent about the uncovering of this potential indifference.

You said the sex of believing is dirt.

You are its immaterial organ.

Your economy did this to you.

You are Lucretian and self-reliant but sometimes exhausted.

Nor is sensing private.

You are neutral, like an event.

Trees, lights, on a level with the genitalia.

You are no longer aesthetical.

A gate made of marble and coat-check stubs.

You are not a colour without having the colour of this red.

On a level with intuitive reason and the complicated history of grace.

You are not the emergency of money.

Last night the parking lot was dreaming the words of your ancestors and enemies.

You are only lyrical if you're harsh.

In expressive range, too, your atmosphere branched out.

You are paid the compliment of being dreamt of.

And the weeping was fed an earring.

You are provisional and unconcerned with the entire feminine machinery.

And the enjoyable gland also dribbles its politics.

You are quite familiar with the iterative terrain.

You are no longer aesthetical.

You are sometimes a confusion of formal levels and sometimes a vicious circle.

You're not spiritual and light either.

You are the crow on Saint Radegund's desk.

You're making a site for error.

You are the silence they exchanged.

Don't warn us again. Don't toot the little horns.

You are then hostile and alien.

You'd like to read a paragraph that's not on the wall.

You aren't a woman.

You would like to have vanished utterly.

You arrive at its diagram, accompanied by a strong aroma of melancholy.

That the snow prevented you.

You ask: what if language is already beyond itself?

You listened to mist.

You asked about love.

Coded, highbrow, late-night.

You assumed a responsibility to disobey.

A gate made of buckets.

You awoke and boiled her dress in ink.

You're aloof to your own extremity.

You became strange, you became her eyes.

Thence to measured earth and its wretchedness.

You became successively a priest, a gambler, a thief, apprentice to an apothecary, a doctor, a clerk in a provincial town.

The dry tree of your task, the citydogs cavorting.

You become the girl who swims underwater.

Your concept is clear: to practice dreaming, then to dream, then to make a record.

You begin to research the anticipatory relation between sensing and fear.

And you have no money, but all of your cruelty is intact.

You believe women exist.

I can't do a thing when I am in your presence.

You believe you are of supple character.

You wanted to make a soul contagion.

You bite into the fruit you invent and it runs down her face.

You will have been recognized by a tree.

You borrowed back some technical defects.

At first you couldn't decide about style.

You breathed for those who dedicated themselves to burning.

You hid as the revolution was being defeated.

You build a catalogue of depletions.

Then you penned a quick imitation on the freedom of stupidity.

You burst to a skirty froth.

Now to enact comically solemn sexual rituals, you said.

You called and got only an echo.

Then psychology reared its battered head.

You came to understand the idea of destiny in this way.

The peculiar indwelling of rime was a roving organ.

You can sense yourself as singular simply because sound is all around you, touching you as a world.

Thus the licking and sleeking of offices.

You can't go back.

And this is the continuous action of the given world on your person.

You carried the great discovery of poetry as freedom, not form.

You see more and more things you want to interpret.

You changed the equation.

Again you store meaning in your body.

You conducted the documentation of a trembling.

And once again you are the one who promotes artifice.

You could never decide about will and using it.

Vicious, vicarious shifters!

You couldn't again submit your own name.

Could you be the historian of the future?

You counted into the problem.

You'll leave the professorate to their concept of paucity.

You craved the diurnal irregularities of the imagining life.

You define 'city' as a viscous sensing.

You decide to meditate on the system of a seam.

At first you want only this tangible surplus.

You decide to reject the concept of absence.

But your theory of rest begins at the horizon.

You decorate time with sprigs and scraps of mortal stuff.

You also have a theory for your saunter.

You define 'city' as a peopled-through sensing.

You make no attempt to govern the fact of duration.

You describe this free gesture of uncertainty.

It is still only noon in your reading.

You devoted yourself in a gentlemanly way to literary pursuits.

You have transferred your being into a possibility.

You did not disappear to yourself.

So now you are an economist.

You did this gravely.

The balance changes, and you care less.

You didn't die.

If you paint with a blushy tint, it's mostly kept for solitary pleasures: napping, smoking, strolling, thieving.

You diligently study the subtext.

With your hands in the pockets of your monumental coat, you strolled across the pedantry of becoming.

You dispel a skein of cloud.

Similarly, that is.

You don't feel obliged to express any gratitude or obedience.

You also take into consideration an element of rarity.

You don't know what a body is.

Your intuition sends messages.

You dream of the cogito, wanting to swim in its work.

A jay, a rook, a parting trinket.

You drift past objects left as wrecks.

A gate made of string and charcoal.

You entered this university of vines and crumpled mosaic, hot sun, the cracks in the walls, the balconies of the university peeling and collapsed.

Now you'll be a whore, now you'll say 'darling.'

You exercise the pleasure of refusal.

Nor are you the custodian of an image.

You expose metaphysics to your organs.

All you wanted was a little bit of accurate description in which to disappear.

You feel minute perceptions speeding across a dirty surface.

I found five hundred solid and nervous words in the margin of your Johnson.

You feel with your own mortality the ruin of a world.

Black mould, animal hair, food, receipts, petals, sloughed skin.

You felt your ears love.

A gate made of a sofa bed and light bulbs.

You felt yourself justified in speaking of cadence.

There you look for what is already institutionally incomplete.

You fling open regret.

There at the creature-riven unfounding, at the sorrow of animals, at the invention of sentiments.

You found music and pleasantness in the copula.

It takes you a long time to shed the specificity of your desires; in actuality the task remains unfinished.

You frequent whatever's supernatural, negative and sexual.

Who will show you the secret to this living as a body?

You go forward until you are stopped, and you are never stopped.

You were numb; you heard a rumour; you twisted in your sleep.

You had a feeling for garments.

You had a feeling for garments.

You had been hoping for better questions.

Certainly you have aspired to thoroughness.

You had believed and argued for each of the theories in its turn.

Also you have aspired to a sincerity of skepticism.

You had drunk only half of the wine.

You'll go to a place that is crumbling in order to watch civilization fall.

You had emigrated from authenticity to truth and the way had not been smooth.

What you see are muzzled speeches and political beliefs.

You had fallen upon the situation where the designation 'speculative' functioned as insult.

You're going way out on a purple raft.

You had more important things to do.

Let feminism be this girl raging at a chandelier.

You had not always been faithful to their miniature world.

The perceiving is for yourself, but meets at no doctrine of the subject.

You had the sensation of bathing in doubt as if it were silence.

You can sense yourself as singular simply because sound is all around you, touching you as a world.

You had thrown yourself into risk without recognizing the act for what it was.

Nor were you fearful of the caesura.

You had wanted to believe that language needs us to witness its time.

You imagine it as bad synthesis or unfinished synthesis or abandoned synthesis.

You have been accused of being a pornographer.

You drift past objects left as wrecks.

You have borrowed impossibility from ornament.

You were mistaken to please.

You have gathered a bundle of rotted sticks.

As years go by, you waste more and more value.

You have here an unfixed being.

It is cause for celebration.

You have invented nothing.

You decide to reject the concept of absence.

You have other doctrines.

Part of your immodesty is opaque.

You have retained most of your original arrogance.

Yet you experience your body as the failing and pulsing civic medium.

You have transferred your being into a possibility.

You would like to reveal the descriptive potential inherent to these organs.

You haven't enough time to believe anything but the comedy of sensing.

I must not believe that you judge on the basis of facts; you judge on the basis of what you are.

You hid as the revolution was being defeated.

About the violet ethnicity: you've always been a dandy.

You imagine it as bad synthesis or unfinished synthesis or abandoned synthesis.

And afternoon passes into evening with the usual ritual uncertainty, and you annotate the skyline making certain to include the word 'apricot.'

You just have to describe what it means.

You've entered into the surplus.

You knew that already, but had once again forgotten.

Perhaps memory is a surface of negative curvature, you muse.

You knew what an animal is.

I don't know how to solve your loneliness.

You learn that lightning shoots upwards, from the earth.

It seems that your data does that.

You left a wake of linguistic sillage.

Like Cuvier smashing the glass jars at the Natural History Museum.

You lie in bed and read Marx.

You borrowed back some technical defects.

You liked to carry out partial recuperations because they were less plausible.

Each of the several rhythmic sequences remains intransigent, and so you make thought with them.

You listened to mist.

Shabbiness, fumbling, elbow grease.

You made your muscles into extremely fine and silky tools.

A gate made of gold, metal rods, driftwood, glass, concrete, peacock feathers, wood.

You make no attempt to govern the fact of duration.

Are you rich?

You meant that by remarkably indirect paths you'd understand one god simply in order to let go of all belief.

Unsorted, unparsed.

You might ask exactly where that sensation of interiority is situated.

You would re-enact the cravat diagrams: L'Orientale, L'Américaine, Collier de Cheval, Sentimentale, À la Byron, En Cascade, De Bal, Mathématique, Irlandaise, Maratte, Gastronome.

You might go so far as to falter.

And then also: Jésuitique, De Chasse, En Valise, En Coquille, À la Colin, À la Paresseuse, À l'Italienne, À la Russe.

You move across the incommensurability of sensing.

At times you love nastiness and bawdry.

You move to the left of the audible range of sound: pine wind in 1800s. Winter night in 1700s. Crickets.

Who will describe your odd survival?

You moved the taxonomy around.

Because you are lazy and voluptuous you lost. And then you applauded.

You need a hat against anger.

At times you indulge in an ostentation of sorrow.

You never agreed with disambiguation.

You had emigrated from authenticity to truth and the way had not been smooth.

You note the smell of rain, bread and exhaust mixed with tiredness.

Now you must return by a different route.

You now no longer use better words.

You move across the incommensurability of sensing.

You offer your substance to an interpretive intervention.

How did you come to be in the vicinity of these sunken pools and chandeliers?

You play and believe within a recurrent sensation.

Now you would be a governess perhaps, with ink-spotted sheets and frayed lingerie.

You play and believe.

Your intellect works only among tactile traces.

You played every card; you had your reasons.

You were annotating the idea of a long elastic present that could include violence and passivity and patience as well as cities, as would a crystal of quartz.

You presuppose a free, opened and unlimited space.

For example, in the noticed friction between thinking and perceiving, your provocation could be built.

You proposed a different emotional education.

Its scale will be wrong in order to announce an illegitimacy.

You pulled over to sleep.

Supernatural, social and divine.

You put on your gorgeousness and yell.

A gate made of artificial plants, vinyl, hinges and pins.

You raised your silk scarf.

You suddenly recognized that for a long time you had been thinking the wrong materiality, that you had inadequately differentiated.

You recalled the driftwood windowsills and tumbling pine cones on the roofs.

Always for you the present is wreckage, or it is the part of a science that does not yet exist.

You recalled the heaviness of blankets in the cabins of 1979.

Intransigence, difficulty and unresolved contradiction.

You recalled the yellow flower called the cuckoo picked for luck in early spring.

A gate made of Perspex.

You receive a similar paucity.

Could it be over already?

You re-emerged confused.

Simultaneously for and against this tradition of minor failure, you have acquired a cummerbund.

You refuse apocalyptic consciousness.

Sometimes you need a record of your life.

The two concepts meet at your refusal.

And then you recline against an image.

You refuse the demand for self-identity in aesthetics or in politics.

With the immediacy of an iamb, you hear a child, a goose, a crow.

You resound elsewhere.

You wanted to be precise because there is the opportunity to be precise.

You rest just to the side of this great, innocent, manipulated faith in the individual will.

In the old clothes market you witnessed your own unweaving.

You rotate away from its sign.

It was spoken, transmitted, temporal, not arbitrary.

You said the market doesn't merit belief.

Allotment machines, irises, lamps, water clocks, laws, indictments.

You said the sex of believing is dirt.

A gate made of poles, stanchions and masking tape.

You said we have both a colony and a god.

And you counted, you counted.

You said you can't evade a binary by turning.

You proposed a different emotional education.

You sallied forth across emptied sidewalks, your fists in your pockets.

What you felt was the movement of sound through your body in its bed in the city not your own but particular nonetheless.

You saw the shadow of the hummingbird and then the hummingbird, from beneath.

That year, all of your muscles became useful.

You say we clothe ourselves against death.

You are arrogant.

You say your health has never been written.

You'll always refute the necessity of shame.

You see creatures of chemicals make some kind of love.

What works then? What works?

You see more and more things you want to interpret.

You assumed a responsibility to disobey.

You see small mammals fighting in trees.

Your prosody of noise will have been misapprehended.

You seem to be an inversion in perception.

No theory is your life, Precious.

You seized the freedom to occupy a vanishing referent.

Nor garret.

You send them back to their diminutive need to identify with everything they see.

In the shabbiness of persisting, the lapsed fibres and the dust, you find an economy to believe.

You sensed your future unfounding.

You lie in bed and read Marx.

You set out from consciousness carrying only a small valise.

Then sleepiness came like an incision.

You shook 'til the little harness flew from her face.

You'll not shame it.

You simply contemplate those russet mountainsides.

An unknowing expands within your pronoun but it feels convivial.

You simply set aside the fantasy of the all-responsible subject.

Perhaps you are the memory of her senses.

You sing to remember.

You take shelter in a figural sensation.

You seek a coat for intellectual ampleness.

Then you are the memory of her dress.

You suddenly recognized that for a long time you had been thinking the wrong materiality, that you had inadequately differentiated.

You decorate time with sprigs and scraps of mortal stuff.

You swam into splendidness.

To whom do you speak?

You take shelter in a figural sensation.

You never agreed with disambiguation.

You think that houses seem to be built entirely of sorrow.

As for the scrappy parking-lot trees, you are full of tenderness for the feminine in them.

You think this place could be worldless.

You want a politics of incompletion.

You think with plants and rags, with prepositional inadequacy, with improvised throat of sorrow.

There you go, there you go, there you go.

You thought that you could take all of the risks.

A gate made of wood.

You tried to remember each hotel room in each town and city and the view from each window over roofs and streets.

You learn that lightning shoots upwards, from the earth.

You tried to see how the sky in 1972 comes up absent.

You don't feel obliged to express any gratitude or obedience.

You twined your whole history of love into a wreath and this was it.

Your sky is fabulous.

You use speech to decorate duration for somebody.

You go forward until you are stopped, and you are never stopped.

You walked beside the wresting and burning of commodities.

Prosody was the house you sketched around your body.

You want a politics of incompletion.

You felt yourself justified in speaking of cadence.

You want a sonic socio-affective structure.

You had not always been faithful to the miniature world.

You want to fill the thought of it with extra existence.

Time is short; you need to constrain your feeling for the sentence.

You want to think about everything open, poor, spontaneous, exposed.

Instead you'll synthesize time.

You wanted me to reach through the continent to the text you were embellishing.

This is what pouring looks like.

You wanted to be intransitive.

You were Maxine, Sally, Catriona. You were Beatrice, Emily, Kathleen, Elaine. You were Olive and Susan.

You wanted to be precise because there is the opportunity to be precise.

You expose metaphysics to your organs.

You wanted to make a soul contagion.

Inextricably you arrive at a weak argument. Impeccably, that is.

You wanted to make your tiredness into a surface.

You simply set aside the fantasy of the all-responsible subject.

You wanted to release priorness.

It took you some time to discover the displacement.

You wanted to say something new about space and forests.

It billows lavishly from a narrowness.

You wanted to see an image that had never been seen.

It's a low-slung rising of a kind of beneficial smoke in the chest.

You wanted to wear the feathered mask of a owl.

You want to think about everything open, poor, spontaneous, exposed.

You weep into a hand.

You have borrowed impossibility from ornament.

You went down the road you were thinking about.

You'd like to say your body is functionless.

You went to the river just to gaze at the river, like an old man.

You called and got only an echo.

You went toward the great experimenters in the domain of longing.

Therefore you transcribed yourself.

You were an intuition without a concept.

You are banality.

You went with your friends to talk.

You devoted yourself in a gentlemanly way to literary pursuits.

You were annotating the idea of a long elastic present that could include violence and passivity and patience as well as cities, as would a crystal of quartz.

You played every card; you had your reasons.

You were being internally photographed.

You raised your silk scarf.

You were hubris and I liked this about you.

The system of relationship you maintained with your body kept dissolving.

You were in the position of perpetual commentary.

You refuse the demand for self-identity in aesthetics or in politics; the two concepts meet at your refusal.

You were Christine, Molly, Lynette. You were Marie, Gwyneth, Oenone, Stacy, Erin. You were Lorna and Allyson.

As for garlands ...

You were mistaken to please.

You felt your ears love.

You were numb; you heard a rumour; you twisted in your sleep.

You might ask exactly where that sensation of interiority is situated.

You were out in a paper boat in the river of the city, listening.

The huge sky over the working harbour felt home-like.

You were out somersaulting in darkness.

You just have to describe what it means.

You were poverty shivering in an old turquoise city.

For you, subjectivity would be about inventing a populated world that exists.

You were reading the city recklessly.

Even the distant hum of cars from the highway overpass.

You were standing outside in your body.

There's an intimacy you want to protect.

You will have been recognized by a tree.

The present is all with you.

You wore the dress as payment.

You want to fill the thought of it with extra existence.

You worked with painstaking fidelity to the documents.

Paperback *Iliad* on the dashboard.

You would educate yourself to an absolute and unconditional submission to the demands of transcription.

Usually you will not have made a decision about how to advance.

You would like thought to release something other than laboratory conditions.

You feel with your own mortality the ruin of a world.

You would like to have vanished utterly.

Some believe you ought to assume a tone of sincerity.

You don't care to reveal the descriptive potential inherent to these organs.

You'd rather hang out and natter in a little food stall.

You would re-enact the cravat diagrams: L'Orientale, L'Américaine, Collier de Cheval, Sentimentale, À la Byron, En Cascade, De Bal, Mathématique, Irlandaise, Maratte, Gastronome.

From your mouth issues a varied stream of flowers: roses, columbines and others.

You would visit the great libraries just prior to their destruction in order to taste the ancient ego nectar.

These new fashions could help you feel hope.

You, with your one-sided headache, your dark relationship to nature, your lack of whatever.

As for the serial description …

You'd like to read a paragraph that's not on the wall.

You begin to research the anticipatory relation between sensing and fear.

You'd like to say your body is functionless.

It remains unachieved.

You'd rather be a dandy than a writer.

You wanted to be intransitive.

You'd rather hang out and natter in a little food stall.

You wanted to wear the feathered mask of a owl.

You'll always refute the necessity of shame.

You wanted me to reach through the continent to the text you were embellishing.

You'll assume that in your century the darkness is necessary.

That they become their deaths, you said.

You'll build a support for the certainty of causelessness.

So you came to nilling.

You'll diss the privative skit called sex.

Then you would be part of the science that does not yet exist.

You'll go to a place that is crumbling.

You have gathered a bundle of rotted sticks.

You'll just speak for prosody from now on.

And your despair is not a philosophic datum.

You'll leave the professorate to their concept of paucity.

You exercise the pleasure of refusal.

You'll not shame it.

This is the annotation of the movement of the site of authority, you think.

You'll see.

Atoms, theatres, famines.

You're aloof to your own extremity.

A gate made of a plinth.

You're also collecting an archive of the absurdity of value.

You put on your gorgeousness and yell.

You're absolutely in love with trees.

You dispel a skein of cloud.

You're fierce, then you're tired.

You were in the position of perpetual commentary.

You're bent to a book as the uprising unfurls.

The countess of prose in your abandoned orchard.

You're finding out about the collapsible body.

I'm for the ennoblement of your curious kind of existence.

You're for the viable infinity of the pelvis.

Authority is speech that does not limit itself to mimicking something that already exists; it is free to deform and invent, as long as it remains obedient to its own inner law, you say.

You're going way out on a purple raft.

Some have deep apartments, some have shallow apartments.

You're good at it.

The question now, you think, is who can really afford this law.

You're in a life-facing position.

Your interior is all exterior.

You're in favour of a potent inhumanness.

Its immateriality is spoken, transmitted, temporal, not arbitrary.

You're in the part of the night where it's quietest.

Thus an hypothesis occurs to you: consciousness is cosmetic, but not in an individual sense.

You're interested in the brutality of description: it is the traversal of this infinitely futile yet fundamental and continuous space called the present.

Still, you're totally in love with subjectivity.

You're making a site for error.

With seemingly insufficient means, you slept, you wrote, you listened.

You're not so spiritual and light either.

Your vocation for research did not abate.

You're the most imitative of all.

You twined your whole history of love into a wreath and this was it.

You're witnessing the belated eruption of a real condition.

Windshield wipers, train crossings, tape loops.

You've also been women.

The form never extinguishes its own irony.

You've entered into the surplus.

You did not disappear to yourself.

Your concept is clear: to practice dreaming, then to dream, then to make a record.

A gate made of forceps and silicone tube.

Your concept remained surface but you didn't yet know why.

Wherever you go, you will be a city.

Your differential was necessary.

A bunch of uncanniness emerges, smelling of foam and violets.

The economy did this to you.

And these phonemes were the phonemes of a perfume that combed your body.

Your errors are colossal.

More collective cosmetics! you decide.

Your face was pure query.

A thumb-sized bird, a medieval allegory, a metaphor that sustains the activity of thinking.

Your feathered hip tutu speaks.

A gate made of cotton, nylon, rubber and leather.

Your fidelity has ceased.

Beneath it the slithering black river.

Your fluid would be spit.

Still there was no solution for the fabulous problem.

Your formal discretion expressed itself in the non-convergence of identity with itself.

The grand law empties you of preference.

Your goodness lifts like a cock.

The I-speaker on your silken rupture spills into history.

Your historical pleasure was metrically interrupted by the inadequacies of terminology.

Then you keep spilling.

Your intellect works only among tactile traces.

You're good at it.

Your interior is all exterior.

Within taxonomy, it quivers and variegates.

Your internal sensation was that of a moving space of surfaces become soundlessly musical.

Already the city you had described was gone.

Your intuition sends messages.

So long, big doors, painted with sea light and honey.

Your misunderstanding stopped just short of thoroughness and this was your particular charm.

Your feathered hip tutu speaks.

Your new skin would be prosodic – that is, both esoteric and practical.

Yeah, fleece and honey.

Your problem is again your own transformation.

The overpass hums in you all night as you sleep.

Your projects and their wrecks and ruins; your dogs.

Again you consider the sumptuous wreckage of the present.

Your pronoun leaks thus.

A girl in a black cotton dress and bare legs is wearing a tiara.

Your sky crumbles open.

Partly vibrant, partly wavering, partly failing.

Your prosody will have been misapprehended.

A gate made of lamps.

Your sky is fabulous.

There was light coming out of your skin.

Your stiff tail is all incipience.

You see creatures of chemicals make some kind of love.

Your subjectivity shouldn't be rationed.

This protocol will show that newness is one of the possible horizons of forgetting.

Your surface is entirely concentric.

You went down the road you were thinking about.

Your thinking is not a market.

Out of curiosity you constructed a model.

Your tradition: the dried-out green bottle fly dangling from a web like an earring.

Carnations and peat moss and a collapsing wall.

Your vocation for research did not abate.

A gate made of carpet tape.

Yours is the prosody of being misapprehended. It has been called shame and has a conventional pronoun.

You changed the equation.

Yours is the social class that disappeared.

You decide to meditate on the condition of a seam.

Yours was a shabby time, and you felt it as such.

How are you distributed across negation?

You seem to remember.

Now listening will be the luminous duration of your tissues.

With the emotional artifice you share with all your class, you step off the curb.

What if there were a life that sustained life?

What if you press the time of the quotidian all over its surface?

You've also been women.

What we have is a mix of improper disclosures of partial information mixed with inaccurate information and then drawn into unfounded conclusions, you said.

You're in the part of the night where it's quietest.

Now only time is wild.

Present: An Index
by Pascal Poyet

(looking for characters)

Again, again, again.
Absolutely, totally, love.
Annotation, authority, apricot.
Anonymous, sense, unfounding.
Arrive, argument, aroma.
Became, becomes, bodies.
Body, hotel, surfaces.
Burning, insult, speculative.
Byron, Byronic, cravat.
Called, culled, picked.
Cause, diss, skit.
Chandelier, feminism, how come.
City, velocity, paucity.
Cock, owls, vultures.
Coded, highbrow, late-night.
Cognition, perception, pause.
Colour, colouration, red.
Commodities, conceptual, sensation.
Condition, distribution, cloud.
Cosmetics, collective, perfume.
Craved, crow, cuckoo.
Description, brutality, place.
Desire, instrument, unfinished.
Disappear, description, category.
Doodle, Venus, pornographic.
Dove, dog, choices.
Dream, dress, difficult.
Duration, luminous, fact.
Economy, economy, economy.
Edges, banality, sensing.
Entire, utterly, vanished.
Erotic, rhetorical, thought.

Error, free, compatible.
Exhausted, narrative, Lucretian.
Existence, intimacy, paperback.
Experience, experimenters, longing.
Exuding, celebrating, cheering.
Fear, feathered, speaks.
Female, feminine, trees.
Form, freedom, irony.
Funny, cosmic, humble.
Fur, destiny, idea.
Future, present, science.
Girl, sun, Nietzsche.
Glands, nerves, politics.
Grateful, gratefully, worse.
History, historical, spills.
Human, tail, incipience.
Idyll, palpability, loss.
Impersonal, ampleness, coat.
Inchoate, infinities, incompletion.
Index, information, irony.
Lady, expression, concept.
Late, late, late.
Law, authority, mimicking.
Life, practice, record.
Lungs, paper, boat.
Machinery, feminine, theatre.
Market, misapprehended, misunderstanding.
Misunderstanding, thoroughness, aspired.
Move into, open, skirty.
Natural, social, intuitive.
Necessary, needed, support.
Noise, prosody, protocols.
Occurs, hypothesis, horizon.
Open, spaciousness, weeping.
Organs, metaphysics, descriptive.
Pages, sound, crickets.

Pictures, private, image.
Pine, perceiving, provocation.
Potential, insistent, hut.
Present, wrecks, aesthetics.
Problem, pronoun, condition.
Profound, time, apartments.
Pronoun, metaphor, leaks.
Prosodic, skin, would.
Question, query, currency.
Reading, city, destroy.
Requires, remain, recognize.
Rhythm, rhythmic, noon.
Route, road, return.
Said, death, clothe.
Saunter, roving, way.
Scrappy, shabby, persisting.
Sensation, sensorium, where.
Sense, sensing, comedy.
Sentence, feeling, garments.
Sex, word, unconvincing.
Shame, sound, procedure.
Shapely, pleasures, solitary.
Silken, social, rupture.
Simply, felt, interval.
Sing, seem, remember.
Site, style, decide.
Skin, light, history.
Skirty, heavy, beauty.
Smudgy, thick, cold.
Sorrow, houses, plants.
Soundlessly, silence, exchange.
Speech, decorate, stuff.
Subject, subjects, subjectivity.
Sunday, precious, life.
Surface, perceptions, shirred.
Surplus, taxonomy, tangible.
System, seam, condition.
Textures, structure, sonic.

Thinking, moving, unknowing.
Time, times, wild.
Tiny, expensive, experience.
Tiredness, procrastination, doubt.
University, swimming pool, botanical
   park.
Uprising, book, bent.
Value, waste, archive.
Violence, passivity, patience.
Wednesday, Thursday, drift.
Witness, ego, eruption.
Woman, women, bored.
Wrecks, wreckage, recklessly.
You, yourself, beginner.

Acknowledgments

My friends have generously helped me realize this book: Hadley+ Maxwell's cover art is only part of a gorgeous series of eight silkscreen posters they made to accompany the text. Poet Stacy Doris, sadly missed, read the manuscript before its submission to Coach House, and Pascal Poyet's deeply engaged editing work developed from a conversational translation process that will result in the publication in France of *Cinéma du présent*. Poyet's translation began when we were invited by poets Sarah Riggs and Cole Swensen to take part in the annual summer Read Hall translation seminar in Paris in 2012. His index was written as a response to the text during our participation in Poets and Critics at Université Paris Est Marne-La-Vallée, a series of two-day colloquia on contemporary poets and poetics, which focused on my work in December of 2012. Thank you to the organizers, Vincent Broqua and Olivier Brossard, and to the other participants, for engaging discussions around the manuscript. Alana Wilcox at Coach House is an extraordinary publisher, and I have been indebted to her since 2006, when we started working together. I am also grateful to the Canada Council for the Arts, the Fund for Poetry, and to Simon Fraser University's Ellen and Warren Tallman Writer-in-Residence program, for support that assisted the writing of this poem, which took place between 2008 and 2012, in Oakland, Berkeley, Vancouver and La Malgache, France.

Lisa Robertson

Books by Lisa Robertson

Poetry

The Apothecary
XEclogue
Debbie: An Epic
The Weather
The Men
Lisa Robertson's Magenta Soul Whip
R's Boat

Essays

Occasional Works and Seven Walks from the Office for Soft Architecture
Nilling: Prose

Typeset in Arno

Printed and bound at the old Coach House on bpNichol Lane in Toronto, Ontario, on Zephyr Antique Laid paper, which was manufactured, acid-free, in Saint-Jérôme, Quebec, from second-growth forests. This book was printed with vegetable-based ink on a 1965 Heidelberg KORD offset litho press. Its pages were folded on a Baumfolder, gathered by hand, bound on a Sulby Auto-Minabinda and trimmed on a Polar single-knife cutter.

Edited by Pascal Poyet
Designed by Alana Wilcox
Cover art, front and four versions of the back selected from a portfolio of eight silkscreen posters produced by Hadley+Maxwell in response to reading the manuscript for *Cinema of the Present*. Their aesthetic is inspired by the political posters created by the Atelier Populaire for the May '68 Paris uprising. All eight are available for sale at chbooks.com/cinemaposters.

Coach House Books
80 bpNichol Lane
Toronto ON M5S 3J4
Canada

416 979 2217
800 367 6360

mail@chbooks.com
www.chbooks.com